# The You That Is Everywhere

# The You that is Everywhere

### Gary Rosenthal

POINT BONITA BOOKS

—for *Amor*

Published by
POINT BONITA BOOKS
5920 Dimm Way
Richmond, CA 94805
fax and tel: (510) 232-1401
toll-free orders: (800) 429-1112

ISBN 0-9665726-0-2
LCCCN: 98-67533

First Edition

Design by Joel Friedlander, Marin Bookworks
Cover image: "The Face in the Wind," J. O. Brubaker, 1907
Cover design: Mark Wagner, www.heartsandbones.com
Manufactured in the United States of America

Cover image copyright © 1998 PhotoDisc, Inc.

# Contents

## II.

# III.

# Preface

It must be that all books, in some way, write their authors—leaving them altered.

This book has to do with the heart, a river which rose unexpectedly, and flooded my banks with poems.

Most of these poems came in a rush, as an almost daily response to a relationship. For months they came, faithfully, sometimes several a day, often waking me in the middle of the night—and then immediately placed in the neighboring mailbox.

Most came in practically whole, which is rare for me—with very little re-write needed, or at the time, possible.

When the relationship seemingly came to an end—as abruptly as it had flared into being—the poems slowed to a trickle. What anguish! And I don't know which I missed more, for it's hard to separate: the human and sacred other, a self in intimate relation to them, the linked reception of the poems.

In the process of receiving these gifts, I feel I came to understand something about the Taoistic sense of integrity (the "Te" in the Tao Te Ching), as well as something mysterious about relationship that Dante and Rumi discovered. Specifically, how another person (Beatrice, Shams, Husam—and the "you" of these poems) can be human and simultaneously more than that, a gate-way into another dimension, another mode of being.

This "gate-way" is the most lofty function of the Muse. Behind the beloved is the Beloved.

Certainly in a Rumi poem, there's a remarkable way the personal and the Universal flow forth from each other. And maybe there's the beginning scent of that mystery in a few of these.

When Rumi found himself separated from Shams he was thrown back on himself, and his grieving was enormous. For he felt cut off—not only from the personal connection—but from the realm of Divine Love that his relationship with Shams had helped him to access. The challenge in Rumi's grief was to find a way back to Love with a capital L.

In the wake of a love that has opened us to a new dimension of depth, it is hard not to feel shabby and haunted when we feel apart from it, haunted by the memory of having once been that open.

For there is a trust in loving, that can become a trust in living. A trust that helps hold and empower an entrance into an intimacy that is shared—not only between lovers—but with the universe itself.

So this book has been a kind of initiation for me. An initiation that hopefully will continue.

I feel grateful to Judith for her extraordinary empathy, radical honesty, and willingness to accompany me on the path as I learn about loving. I feel graced as well by her acceptance of the wild varieties of clunkyness that show up when my love does not.

When these poems first began to come in I read a few to my teacher in *dokusan*—the formal Zen interview—which with him is seldom very formal. He then grabbed me by the shoulders and—with what seemed at the time an ideological bit of *chutzpah*, said: *"this is what Zen has needed—to marry with the Troubadour tradition of ecstatic, romantic love."*

And later, in the candle-lit semi-darkness of the interview room during retreat (when I was confused about my practice), he pulled out a yellow legal pad, drew something on it—and handed me the sheet of paper saying, *"this—following this—is your practice."* On the sheet of paper was drawn a large heart.

So I feel gratefully fortunate for the enheartenment of John Tarrant, *Roshi*—as well as for the guiding presence in my psyche of Rumi, Dante, and the troubadours.

This must be what ancestors are for.

—G.R.
Earth Nest Ranch
July 1, 1995

*I.*

# Wild Hooves

The love poems
I want to write
had not been lived...


Embarrassed, I now want
                    to burn,
                    sweep,
                    erase
            all evidence
            of how I've loved before...


And the crust
that had covered
my heart?


        *trampled*
                *by wild hooves*
                        *of your beauty*

# The Pine Cone

Who knows why
its time has come
to fall?

       But in its one
       crunchy, spiny
       sap-drip life

   a pine cone
         clunks
            & clunks
               & clunks
its way down
from the high trees

  It hits on many
         branches
  as it falls

  Each branch
  seems to hold it
  in wooden arms
        for the briefest of interludes
      pausing
         the inevitable
      final
       & true embrace
    with the ground
    from which all earthly things
come

& return...

        I, who do not easily
                  fall
     clunk
        & clunk
              as I hurtle toward you

      —I did not choose it
     it is simple
         cellular obedience

     as the pine cone, in its time of falling

and you...
a branch—or my earth nest ground...
you will have me—or not...
        either way, my heart

             crashes open

# Lips of October

They've grown plump with presence
a pair of them living together
at the entrance to your face

Gatekeepers, the faithful
& voluptuous servants
in your employ...

Out of their intimate life together—
    meeting to share a wetness,
    a taste, a word, a sound
—they now want a life of their own
                              & to travel!

        *Leaving the known, we return home*
October lips, the salmon are moving upstream
        October geese, your lips lift
                              into the great sky

        "*I want...I want...*" —their simple words
        sound like a kind of honking...

And the wise animals who know

        how to find their way home a thousand miles,

    when the wise animals inside us
                              want to meet
they disappear...

into the alive darkness
                        that descends
                                    facelessly
And I want to follow them...


                and meet you
                        in miraculous blackness
            without a name, a past, a plan...


        Lost, and at the same time, deeply found
        I want to move with you
                        into the slippery current
in a country without maps or road signs
where only
            a familiar rightness guides the journey


                                    & letting go
                        is the only
            means of travel

# How It Happens

years of sitting in the zendo
on a round, black cushion
where the roshi says,

> *"it arises from the heart*
> *& covers heaven and earth..."*


now, gazing at you
Gary says,

> *"it arises from your smile,*
> *the way you move in your clothes*
> *& lift a fork*
>
> > *that opens my heart to all things..."*


—both of these versions, obviously from wind-bags...


Nonetheless,
I know what I know

# Gary's Love Secrets

For no reason you can understand
love arrives riding a bicycle
one day right where you live
(the most unexpected neighborhood of all)

It's like the guy who once caught a lunker bass
using his bologna sandwich for bait
(think of it, a true lunker, happens so rarely
—he's held to this method ever since...)

Since people come to me anyhow
                              for love advice
I thought I'd jot down these few tips
—just some things to bear in mind
if nothing else is biting...

Remember:
        —no reason...
        —no understanding can account for it...
        —it's always unexpected, close to home
                              as likely as any...

And the last thing (which may prove unimportant)

        —watch out for bicyclists...

        (& anything that moves,
        that moves your heart, that is...)

—of course, the last item could also be the secret
ingredient...

Like the guy said, who caught the great fish,
using his bologna sandwich for bait,

*"I don't know much, but it worked for me..."*

# You Pinch Yourself. It's Not A Dream

It's like a miraculous restaurant
suddenly opens for business
in your very neighborhood
only the bill never arrives
the food comes
without having to order
& even when the chef's on vacation
its marvelous!

You relax and a dish appears...
You relax, trust some more...
invisible hands start serving your heart's desire
& even the platter it comes on is beautiful!

The reality police
send out an inspector, a street-wise vet
who knows the score, along with somebody from
licensing, whose brother does restaurant reviews...
"altered state..."       "dual-unity wish fulfillment..."
"other-worldly salad dressing..."
They've all got theories, but nobody knows.

Meanwhile, the edges in your voice have softened
something's coursing through your body
that's mellowing you out
nothing manic, just a simple happiness
that feels gentle and content. Things seem easy
and you lose track of time.

How can this be? You're not on drugs...

How long can this last? Your questions seem feeble, insincere, lacking in faith...
You pinch yourself.
It's not a dream.

# Remember

This is getting serious—she's asked for your phone number
so remember, when she wants to find out
how it was to be married to me,
that the stakes are high, given the infrequency
that I fall in love—so give her a good report!

—recollecting all the swanky places I took you
with the classy views, our vacations
—mountains, rivers, lakes...
you can use your discretion

about the tent and the snoring
(& I don't think the fishing part of these times together
is absolutely required for the discussion
—besides, every time I checked in on you
you seemed to be having a good time,
loving nature as you do)

Should she ask about my fidelity, please remember
that for all my poet's views about free love,
how infrequently I actually strayed

Remember how much you liked my earthy, touchy-feely-ness,
and that other thing—bigger and better than most!
(should she ask, just between girls)

You don't have to lie about my house-keeping
—she already knows, though I've lacked gumption
to either clean or show her the upstairs
(you might point out, that there are great impulses
that move through me, that regrettably,
don't allow me to spend as much time with the vacuum

cleaner as I would otherwise wish... but I'm a team-player
who can rise to the occasion & meet standards
if someone else will only set them

Recall—I never hit you—even in the days
when you were drinking & could get abusive
though once I did carry & dump you
out of the house, locking the door. But even so, recollect

I've always been there for you
emotionally, even now, ten years later, when you need
to talk, or some of that wise, heartful counsel
I'm so good at

More than anything—being a woman,
she's gonna want to know about my prospects
for commitment & partnering—and here I truly
have changed for the better—my time alone
has deepened my yearning for someone to love
& grow old with—this is really true,
you won't be leading her astray...

So sweetheart, don't be catty or competitive
but wishing me well, tell her how lucky she is
to have found me, now that I'm entering my peak
let her know how fantastic and rare she must be
for me to be so goo-goo,
that you've never seen me like this before
in all the days since we broke up

Remember—this means a lot
remember—cause I need your help
remember me well—for old times' sake...

# What The Walls Say

There's hand writing on the walls
in fact all of the walls
are filled with this gossip

The walls say:
> *This—is what a burning house is like:*
> *you can't live there. Or barely talk anymore.*
>
> *Though cut flowers, still fragrant, are inside*
> *it will always be a burning house*
>
> *—leave!*

You come to other
walls who say:
> *this—is what home could be*
> *there's dust in rooms you haven't even seen...*
>
> *but notice:*
> > *the wild garden*
>
> > > *that is waiting for you...*

# While You're Considering...

If you wanted to try out
having two boyfriends,

Whats-his-name could have
what he's always wanted

—you, no commitment,
the "freedom" of other women...

I'd have a dazzling lover
—who's not fully here...

And you'd be half-baked:
a runny pie, cut in half

clinging...
to two plates

# I Think Of Other Women

I think of other women—

a long

      pathetic,

           erotic

                career...


Then, thinking of you—

  feel I'm being

          punished

              healed

                  blessed

all—at the same time!

# Scraps & Crumbs

Everywhere I see people
settling
      in relationships
for less than they want

—compromising
what shouldn't be compromised—

for fear of being alone...

No! Great Love requires *sacrifice!*
not something puny
like "compromise"

*I'll have the whole meal*
*or go to bed hungry!*

# The Ring

*Sacrifice*
          means
                    *to make sacred*

—you draw
          a line
                    a ring

you give
          up
                    everything

else
          to have the heart's
                    deeper desire...


          a gold thing gained
          by what you lose,

          a subtle magic
          in what you choose


For out of the Empty
          center
of the ring

          *Something comes...*

                    my love

          it sings

# What The Body Remembers

There are gestures
which must surely come
from the 12th Century

       —my body remembers them...

The 12th Century
when Romantic Love
first entered the West
—heart time of troubadours...

And I too feel a certain kind of love
entering my heart for the first time...

    —though this is not exactly true
    there was a girl...
              her name was Camiliar Buckley
    it was raining. It was 1956, and I waited—

(in the Love of the 12th Century, one is always
                             waiting...
    & in the time of waiting,
    the time of being apart
    from the beloved—that's when many
    of the purest feelings come

I waited
for Camiliar Buckley to emerge from 2nd grade
so I could carry her over a mud puddle,
throw my jacket down before her feet

      & I did


Waking up this morning,
thinking of seeing you next
I see myself taking your hand
& dropping to my knees, an instinctive worship
the body somehow remembers to do

    —these gestures seem a bit hokey
    in the 20th Century


      —but they are pure
             I assure you
                  Milady...

# Because They Live In It

Because they live in it
        intimately
           suffering
             & learning its love,
   the Eskimos have names
   for fifty kinds of snow...

Because they know
no other
life not watery,

     salmon can steer
        toward the fragrance
           of their Original Home...
There's a marriage
of love & discernment
called *wisdom*
       —but I have no name for *this*
       ...at least not one...

—it's not exactly
     *Agape*
     *Physical*
     *Philadelphian*
     *Romantic*
        —these names all fit in a box
          mailed to us from another time...

My love for you
is being invented...

constantly...

        in some workshop
                from which all things come

    Just now, traffic
    is saying one of the names,

    water, first gushing
    from a hose, is another...

    In sunlight, these bushes, radiate
    only a few
            thousand arms

of the You that is everywhere

            *huntress*
                *who tracks*
                    *me down*

# In Times Of Flood—
# Even The Tao Overflows

There's a river
—and I believe in it—
that flows
            through the middle of the valley
between hills of yes and no...

It finds its way
                by gleaming
                            boulders
                                    of rightness
promising
            neither
too much, nor too little...


        Facing you
        —even when alone—
        *the current, rising...*

                tributaries of moan
                cry
                    & whisper
        enter my voice

                    *unmoored, the tiny boat*
                            *carried away...*

# The Gift

When someone loves you
the way I love you
it's more than personal—
*the Great World*
*is giving*
*one of its finest gifts,*

a fragrance that lingers
on the fingers
of both giver & receiver
in fact, you can't
really tell them apart

This love comes from
Somewhere Else
and when someone loves me
the way you love me
*the Great World*
*is giving*
*one of it's finest gifts...*

# Guests

All day, sacred animals

    visiting from another realm...

        and they're becoming more ecstatic!


And I'm crying...

    *thank you!*
        *thank you!*

## understand this:

*I'm on fire!*

*And don't **want** to be saved!*

# While You Were Away...

I'd rather
make love with you
                in my mind

than with anyone
else
        in the flesh

                So I do...


                coming
                        on and on!

                —I had to will its stop...


    Now
        I put on
    the outfit you dressed me in

                when last I left your door


only three more days
                in this uniform
                        & you'll be home again...

# How Could This Be?

*How could this be—*

that at my age
I've become a virgin

& write love poems
                    for the very first time?

*How could this be?*

that now I love like a water-fall:
giving everything away
                    without being diminished...

*How could this be?*

that when the Great World
wants to give one of its secrets
it hides all else
                    making even heaven & earth disappear...

Since this is the case...

*How could this be—*

that you love me back
and hold me
like the banks of a river

and yet—
            *still sleep*
                        *with another?*

# Out of the Blue

Just a few weeks before
I fell in love with you
I had a dream I had fallen in love
which seemed out of the blue
in the morning, making no sense...

Coming back from a concert
in some shabby neighborhood
of the soul, the woman I'd been loving
decides to get back together
with her old boyfriend, a rich Arab

Filled with grief, some unknown
older people approach me,
*"this is what we were trying
to tell you about her..."*

Now, when I get scared
of losing you to whats-his-name,
scared I'm ignoring a warning
& overwhelmed by a love come out of the blue,
I tell the dream.

Your son's asleep, we're on the couch,
having passed through many hall-ways
of vulnerability, to be in this
spacious intimacy we share...

You listen to the dream, pause,
then say of the woman,

*"sweetie, that's not me..."*

But the truth is
nobody knows what will happen, or when...
in love, you take your chances,
happy to have them, knowing
someday everything's going to vanish,
as if, *back into the blue*

& what makes it easier, is
it's not like I have a choice
to make, when it comes to loving you

# To The Core

Let's take off these clothes!
then—fling aside
mind, bones & hair

At the core
all things
are truly naked

To the core...
come,
meet me there

*II.*

# I Like It

I like it when the room gets rich
with Presence, like a great wine
that's been cellared, and uncorked
enters air for the first time in years

                  & one senses
                              *nobility,*
                                         *the King*
                                                  *has returned...*

I like it when the Love Energy enters your face
and ageless, it dissolves
                              all
                              but the Essential You...

I like it when natural vow-making
enters, exalts the heart
                        & *sacrifice* ...seems
                        like the kinkiest pleasure!

And though it's simple, I like it
when you tell me you love me
for there are times I need reassurance
and then, can't hear it enough

# Your Koan For The Day

Sweetheart, do you know about monkeys?
They love two things almost equally
& it gets them in trouble!

They love their free life
                                    swinging in the trees
but they're addicted
                        to a certain kind of fruit...

Hunters of monkeys
                        place the fruit in jars
                                            attached to a rope

Reminiscent of that other parable—"the eye of the needle,"
the mouth of the jar
is just big enough
                        for the monkey's hand to slide in
but not big enough for the fist to emerge
still grasping the unattainable fruit...


Love without discernment
winds up in a cage

There are bananas
& there are bananas

in a jar—monkey mind
can't tell the difference

                        *the hunters are approaching*
                        *—what will you do?*

# Be Prepared To Lose

If you want
to hedge your bet
go to a race track

If you want
a great Love
*be prepared to lose*

your shirt...
          your heart...
                    your mind...

# It's Not Enough To Ask For Help

You performed ritual
                    magic
...asking like that...
                    & the asking must have been pure,
steeped with longing...


—a beautiful woman
—in her heart
—longing from the core
                    —not even God could refuse that one!


So almost at once—uncanny,
the Mystery places your request
            right in front of your face

        And now you want
        to agonize a decision?

                    What will the Mystery think
                    next time you send up
                    one of your balloons?


Under the talons of imperial Rome
a people yearn for a prophet, a guide

        and miracle of miracles:
        *he appears*      —but it almost never looks
        like we think it will
        —you know this story...

& some are still waiting!

Bad poems often have a moral:

It's not enough to ask for help,
for what your heart truly desires

*you must be faithful*
*when the change has come*

When Mary Magdalene followed Jesus
                              Home,
she too had a history
                    & people must have whispered
when she alone
                    he would kiss on the lips
but the truth is
                    from the moment he appeared
she became a virgin again
                              & his greatest disciple


Officially you're still with another—
so we've been making love
                              for weeks
without taking off
                    a single stitch
—do you think you're being faithful
                              to either
just because you keep
                    your tongue in your mouth?


Two boats are leaving the port
the relation
                    ship of appearances
and the Mystery ship

They go to different places
and one you've already been

# Lost in Translation

The realm
         Love and poetry
                 comes from
is vast
    & domeless

        like someone

           who's lost the top of his head!


How the world holds it
is another matter...

        A true King is born
               in a stable
        He grows up
            wisely
        —writing nothing down...

           Yet his words
                appropriated
        by con-men & bureaucrats

20 centuries pass...
Another true Monarch
wanders this world an exile
—they've taken his country away
& we all watched it happen

but this isn't really about Jesus
or the Dalai Lama—

If this love too
            falls
on stony ground

      it must be that God Herself
      is a poet
                  & Her uni
                        verse fated

                              — *lost in translation*

# *Te*

Years with my teacher...
I've learned
        a single word
one word only—

                *but it flows*

                      *through everything*

*II.*

In times like this
            the easy
    man in the street
               ordinary reaction
        would be
            to close down the store

but because
I've learned

        a single word

I don't...

*III.*

holding it
         all
in love,
      I myself
am held...

            *you will do*

                  *what you do*

# Karma

I've had three Zen teachers
each
      held up a lantern
when I was lost in my woods...


With the second
             koans seemed easy
—she was lenient...
               & when we merged
I could read her mind...


The first one
            would only talk to me
about poetry & girls...


Now, twenty five years
             have passed
so guess what we talk about?

—*I'm completely different*
—*nothing has changed*

# Simeon In Egypt

... Joseph's brothers
      —the very ones who sold him
            into slavery, years before
        are forced into Egypt, seeking grain
          in a time of famine...


...By now Joseph has risen
            to prominence, holds
the favor of the Pharoah,
        and it is with him
the brothers must deal
      to get the grain....

               *My need & desire for you*
               *begins to scare me...*


     —I've always made sure
     it was a seller's market

              & I the seller
*But here I'm the buyer...*

& you could walk
      away from the deal...


        ...Joseph puts Simeon into prison
    as a hostage, and sends the others off
to bring back Benjamin....*Nobody knows Joseph's true Heart...*

...Before I met you
I didn't know
my heart was in exile...

        —Now that I do, like Simeon, I fear
        being left, not knowing

        how this will turn out, a prisoner
        in a land with unfamiliar customs

        *where you hold the keys*

                *as well as the grain*

# In Praise of Penia

In the Ancient World
when they knew
what we must
still discover

**Need** was called *Penia*

She was the mother
of Eros...

...at the root
of our penis...


Until we show
our need
we are still hiding

our root

behind leaden trousers


Eros, yet to be born...


I want to praise *Penia*
for the transformative
*vulnerability* ...

that gives birth
to the heart's
sweet gift

# This Is What It's Like

—you know you're an idiot
but like it better this way...

—your heart is a buoy, for once
in the middle of the channel

& when a ship passes
you know it first hand...

—not exactly *dumb*—it's just that
what you know is very simple...

—you're way back
in the ground, from which figures emerge...

—you could write the intimate biography
of a box of raisons, a bar of soap...

—it's like you've had two histories
all along—and the other,

(the clever one)
had grossly miscalculated...

# Ask The Idiots

I don't know anything
about this—and neither
do the doctors...

To understand this affliction
you must turn
to the patients

And they sound crazy!

They jabber about an ambush,
the weather, a cloud
from which everything comes

How the sun
has fallen into a black lake
(they point to their chests)

Like children, they laugh
& cry a lot

(All agree) it makes no sense
that before the world
was upside down

And this
is right-side up

# The Power of Legitimate Suffering

There's something like a hole
                        in the ground
        of the soul—

        like a root canal, a wound...

        —though in avoiding it
        Essence seems farther

So this time you jump
                    in

                —your face falls off
first, then your voice,
& the rest of
                the shell you've been wearing

Like the Bardo, loving arms
await you...

But first you fall
feeling younger & younger

till you come out
the other side

with your original eyes

# In The Biblical Sense

Like the belly of a whale
we're parked
               in the huge old Buick

    both of us feeling about sixteen
    though the year is 1994


    You tell me there's
             head knowledge
             heart knowledge
               belly knowledge

You say sex
        for you
is like meditation
          for me
—there are things
              that appear to you then

    *knowledge, you haven't felt ready for*


    And then...
          you start
             to kiss me...

# Rapprochement:
# The Maiden Voyage

You kiss me
                then scurry back
afraid of losing
                a harbor...


The infant, afraid
                no one will be there
if she crawls toward the rattle
                of her own desire,
returns to the frustrating mother...



Now I see why
                you settle for so little
& what you want
                seems to elude you


It's not that your ship
                has yet to come in—

You're just too frightened
                of claiming your own life
to ever sail from shore

# The Dummy Of Schizoid Process

There's a dummy, a disembodied
idol
about 12 feet high
that people sometimes carry around
So bulky, it blocks the light of your inner sky...

It's about as much bigger than you
than your mother seemed
when you were a child

And sometimes we spend years
serving the dummy, putting the rest
of the soul on hold...

...or needing to get away
from others, feeling lonely
for our real selves, whom we left
to pick up the dummy

—the dummy
whose demands have grown so exacting,
yet whom seems safer
than being totally alone

Inevitably there come The Compromises
with the dummy, such that we might
never be too smotheringly
close            to another            nor too far,
not fully in
relationship, nor exactly out

as if something might still be left
if we gave only half of ourselves away...

It's not long before everyone
is confused with our dummy

The whole thing sad
                              & confused
like much that happened
when we were young

Sweetheart, *if only you'd give up this insane embrace*
there'd be someone more real
                              & better to hug

in your bed tonight!

# Clueless In San Francisco

...The news is still hitting me
& I'm falling
        down a deep well
though walking with you
           up Buchanan Street
under a cold, white, winter moon...

The intimate, warm little restaurant
at the corner of Greenwich
        turns us away
it's late on Friday night
—we're now 0 for 2, in seeking out
           a place to talk...

You say you have no sense
        of direction
  & make bad choices

& we both know      it is more
than the streets of this city     & its eateries
you are talking about

Again, I am astounded
*how could this be*
      *that you **know** this*
about yourself, but can't stop the machinery
that is taking you away from me...

My sense of the Tao
      recently, has begun to develop—

I look up and notice
                    the motel sign on the corner
knowing a good choice when I see one...

but you don't have this sense
                         except for your witchy
instinct for parking spaces
so I say nothing...
                    ...You are, undeniably, beautiful
a beautiful woman
                    who makes bad choices,

a walking tragedy for all concerned

                    beneath your darling
                                   knitted
                                         hat

# Taking Stock At Winter Haul-out

If love leaves because a woman
                              vanishes
this just means
                    there's more work to do...


        —with this blue face
        from boat's bottom
                          paint & dust
        I must look like Krishna


                              crying
        over you


                There must be a country for this
                grief, a country-western
                                    song at least


        but I'm too tired
                        & depressed
        to even put on
                        another coat


            —on my back, again
            in the shipyard


                            beneath a needy boat

# DABDA

*we could have had it all*
*this is just stupid*
*what a loss!*


A giant foot
        with reptilian scales
                on the leg

    stomps on the love-ground
                compressing the chest
                into a rocky fossil


    —maybe this is how
    the Grand Canyon was formed...


Kubler-Ross says there are stages
of grieving—

    **D**enial
    **A**nger
    **B**argaining
    **D**epression
  & **A**cceptance

        In the country of grief
        the land is arid, covered with bones,

a few stunted trees—
         & I find no order at all

    just border skirmishes
    between these little fiefdoms
    which daily I enter

        all but for one...

# Pluto

Sometimes a god
grabs you by the shoulders
& works you over
for a season or two

And while you are
in his grasp, dragged
beneath the earth
& being replanted
      like a seed,

          all the streams
          of life
      subtly change their course
      & you no longer know
      the way back home

*What you couldn't change*
*the god was doing for you*

while you were suspended
& helpless, the plaything
      of Something enormous...

*What colossal faith*
  *it would take*
    *to say **yes** to this too—*

*not quite dead to the old*
  *nor alive*
    *in the new*

# Love's Double Whammy

When you fall
　　　　in love

the holes in your soul
　　　　　　*suddenly fill with gold!*

& you think: *forever*
　　　　　*you'll be carried*
　　　　　　　　*on the back of a magical pony*

　　　　　This lasts
　　　　for a while...

But this gold
　　　　& pony
　　　　　　*belong to no one...*

When the fall-out comes:
　　　　　*all the gold disappears*
　　　　　—we don't know where—

　　　*& the pony is nowhere to be found...*

Even worse:
　　　those holes
　　　　　in your soul
　　　　　　　begin again to ache!

# The Other Face

They say
            love is blind
                        & merely emotional
                                    love, the love
            of the ego,
                        turns into its opposite...


I say
      not loving is blinder

nonetheless, when you gaze at the beloved
                        try sometimes to see

                  the face that comes without a promise
                  the one that's not for you
                  the face that isn't free

      When we are "betrayed"
      the other face comes forward,
      the one in your eager loving
                        you ignored
      and did not want to see

# Epitaph

*I loved well a haunted beauty*
*I thought that we might wed*
*She wore her chains like promises*
*She chose her chains instead*

*The want she held most deeply*
*The same, her deepest fear*
*She briefly kissed it when it came*
*Then tossed it on its ear*

*Every love deserves an epitaph*
*And some need two or three*
***The way I loved her*** *was the gift*
*That lingers now with me*

*III.*

Now that I'm better
                    at loving
I become aware of you
                    in a new way...

And you are
                    beautiful...
                              mysterious...
                                        & dangerous...
                    hideous & holy...

present
          yet elusive...

a powerful lover
                    who at other times
          could care less...

                    What a challenge!




                              Judith is gone...


          *tonight*
                    *I'm in love*
                              *with the Nameless*

# Forswearing All Others

After days of going home
                    with every sleazy
                              & indulgent impulse
tonight I'm finally
              desperate    enough to refuse
                                    *everything,*
                    every event
but the marathon
              pursuit through black space,
this obliterating longing
              for the You that seems mysterious
    & far away


—then, empty of thoughts, when the wind
                    & every nearby sound
is finally saying your name,
                    I pretend not to notice...

I'm tired of words
                    & the one who's been speaking me
    even silence
    isn't silent enough

I've absolutely had it
with my security schemes,
              all the numbers
                         I write down on paper
    —if you want me broke
    and broken, and block every doorway

maybe that's because
                    cornered, and sinking

I'm finally ready to meet you...

        In this fierce longing
        I begin to feel clean again

# The Voice & Its Holder

What I miss most is not exactly physical
but someone to hold
                        the heart's true voice


—the one fallen
                        beyond hope

—grounded
                        beneath pretense



I suppose that's part
                        of what God is for...



The voice & its holder, a matched set
                        intimate as your happiest
                                    married friends

Coming home to them
            is like sliding down
                        into an old pair of jeans,

    tasting again
                        the chest's timeless honey

# Deep Inside You

You've finally left him
& want me back

You say I live
deep inside you

& want more from me
than just to be friends...

The Tao is mysterious
& if you're patient enough
even hilarious

    *deep inside you*

        —I'm almost hypnotized
        by the sound of that

        but respond calmly
        at first—with reserve,
        not wanting to appear too eager...

My famous reserve—
alone with you again
—lasts all of three minutes!

# Is It Strange?

While you were gone
my heart
       was wearing a shell

& I obsessed about things
that were *really* stupid,
not just
       quirkily endearing

Then I know it's you
the instant before
I hear the phone ring...

Is it strange
to regard your lover
as a kind of god?

Or is not doing so
the thing that is strange?

# It

We're like the
window, it
is like the wind

Or we're the
flower, it's
the bee

—it does what it does...

& our opening
is where we all
meet


Call it
     "The Third Body,"
"The Guest,"
          or set a place
for it at the table
            & call it
"Elijah"


*a familiar*
       *Other*
          *enters*


my love for you

# Like Bamboo

Tired
        & not even horny,
the joy of being
              next to you
turns me on!

We try it
without hands
          & arms
—all the tree's sap
falls down
to the root

Then we go blind
—the sense of touch
grows only keener

This love is like bamboo
that's escaped from its
container

Sleeping together,
the candles
blown out

—still,
*these* moths
circle the flame

# The Others

Fruit was ripening
                    in the summer heat
all that time
            I loved you in fever
  without removing
                    so much as your blouse...

Then, in that burning
                    you
                        were with Another
—no, not *him*
            but the one who was
  waking
        in back of me...

'Twas good we didn't
                    pick the fruit too soon
  while the sugars were
                    rising
                        into the limbs
so many poems
            flowed in on that tide
of sweet arising
            & it must be the
            Other
                    we thank for them...

Now, alone with you
we make love
almost every night

I wouldn't trade it!

Still, sometimes I miss
                    the Other
who stands behind me
                    not of this time
                    & not of this earth

For when he is here
                    it is possible
                            to meet the Other
                                    woman

            that One
        who stands

in back of you

# What Did I Do To Deserve It?

What is the Source of this luck
—that a woman so
beautiful
        undresses
& gets into bed with me?

loving me loving me loving me

—*what did I do to deserve it?*

Like the kind mother
                of retards,
God must still love Her idiots!

# Totally Ditto

In this stage of loving
we totally agree
as my love for you
                    replies
to your love for me

It feels like devotion
when I give up
                    my familiar ways
to eat what you eat—even *kale*

And when it scratches your face
off goes the beard!

One day, the things
that will drive me crazy
                    about you
will no doubt drive me crazy...

But for now—when I leave you
I want to do so
                    on my knees
crawling backwards

                              kissing the ground

# Nuts

There's someone in me
who doesn't taste right
—there's a thin crust

                with an off flavor
perhaps caused by fear

Even so, if one of us
seems like an idiot

              that's only the shell
& not

     the sweet nut

inside

# Sobering Up

Feeling love's extravagance,
I want to announce
the it I am in
        with you
is so vast
        it leaves the clock
the calendar, the map

*Will you come with me?*


Then, more sober—
everything imaginable
will come into our path:

whirlwinds, other loves
ghosts, initiations,
death
       & other silences

But still—

*Will you come with me?*


Finally, I wake
between your body
& the voice
       a dream has left behind:

*"sleep lovers...*
*the path is long—*

*and real work*
*only begun..."*

# To Meet The King

There's a voice that holds us
though sometimes
we only hear little snatches...

I had a dream the other night
& woke in your arms
remembering only
            the voice
which came at the ending

    Then, this morning, the voice again:

            *"And so we wait for dawn
            to meet the King
                        whose life
            does not end with ending..."*


        However garbled or infrequent,
                                it is good
            to hear such a voice,
            like a message from Home

    —to know they haven't
    forgotten us there
                    though most of each day
    I forget
    I'm living in a Mystery
                & feel unfaithful
    and distracted

In the world behind this one
there are two kinds of kings
                    —One rules a narrow
                    failing realm
                    & his dying
                    seems to go on
                                        forever

—the other kind of king
is just forever
                    & he knows the way
                    to the rest of your life


When I think of the many,
he speaks from the One

When I think of the many
kinds of idiots I've been

he must be what leads
away from all this idiocy

                    *How do we meet him?*

                    Just breathing in this question—
                    something superficial
                    seems to go away

                    & something
                    *every* thing is a part of
                    seems to draw closer

# The Mysterious Question

The mysterious question
returns us
to the Mystery

It is a sheep-herder
that drives away wolves,
wool, the hill-side itself

*to keep having this love*
*we need three things...*

but **which** three
keeps changing

# Bait For The Beloved

Lovers get thick & disappointed
when they take each other
too literally

    This is like filling up
    on the soup & bread
& forgetting
        what the chef is really famous for

You, with your watery ways,
flaky scales & wild sweet flesh
me, like a flashy plastic lure
trolled through the ocean

One kind of metaphor
becomes bait for another
             With this mix of substance
             & illusion
our longing here
        keeps getting hooked
& doesn't make it
        back to the Source

They say tortured vines
make the best wine

    —my shallow rocky soil
    may have a purpose:

*notice how your roots*
*are going deeper*

The thin
            though tasty soup
brought out before the entrée,
a satisfaction that ingeniously
is *meant* to be partial
                    while it whets the appetite
for what's to come

Meanwhile, behind closed doors
someone is busy in the kitchen...

There's another course,
                    another Romance
waiting behind this one—

*Let's love **this***
*while we remember **that***

# The Harbor Buoy

You are telling me
what is missing...

It is nothing new,
just the beginning
of a conversation
　　　　　women have wanted
to have with men
　　　　since God knows when...

—I don't defend myself, just listen,
holding you, till you
begin to cry...

Sometimes it is better
to just hold steady
& make rhythmic
soundings
　　　　　deep in the chest

For I want to be
the harbor buoy
meeting you

　　　　　when you sail off

& come back in

# Two That Held Fast

The apples

—like love itself

*golden*
        *delicious...*


                another Autumn,
                you've disappeared...

    *the uncollected harvest*
                bruised & rotting on the ground


But behind dusty leaf,
        almost hidden,

a pair
        that managed
                to hold fast
                        to the tree
    longer than the rest,

                extracting still
                        from their Source
                the lingering sugar
                        that moves in the limbs

—these Survivors

may be
the fruits of love's *stamina*...

golden & firm

    *almost*
        *unbearably*
            *sweet*

# Acknowledgments

Thanks to Joan Sutherland, *Roshi* and Noelle Oxen-handler, editors of *Blind Donkey*, and Gary Gach, editor of the Parallax Press anthology, *What Book!? Buddha Poems from Beat to Hiphop*, for first publishing some of these poems. "The Gift" was first published as part of a Sufic wedding liturgy for the marriage of Jay and Cathleen Daley. And a somewhat surprising acknowledgment goes out to the numerous other wedding ceremonies in which a number of these poems somehow found employment while the book was still in manuscript.

Point Bonita Books

Going out—or coming back from the sea—it is Point Bonita and its lighthouse—not the more famous landmark, Golden Gate Bridge—that marks the true entrance into either San Francisco Bay—or open ocean . . .

Immediately beyond Point Bonita, seaward, lies the infamous "Potato Patch" (Four Fathom Bank)—where silt deposited for millennia by the Bay and its inland tributaries has formed a shallow bar (in places only four fathoms deep) subject to extreme tidal turbulence . . .

Many ships have sailed around the world only to go down here. And when the bar is breaking, the fishing fleet will approach Point Bonita before making its determination, whether it is possible to get out at all . . .

Point Bonita is thus a liminal space in the physical and archetypal geography of this region. From this Point, one will journey into an increasing sense of danger, adventure, or homecoming . . .

From here, passage through invisible depths and channels will be granted or denied—all based on elemental forces, largely beyond our control . . .

If you would like to be placed on our mailing list, receive free future catalogs, order books—or respond to this one, please write:

Point Bonita Books
5920 Dimm Way, Richmond CA 94805
www.pointbonitabooks.com
fax or tel. (510) 232-1401
toll-free orders (800) 429-1112